Books by Catherine Edwards Sadler

Two Chinese Families (*with Alan Sadler*)
Treasure Mountain: Folktales from Southern China

TREASURE MOUNTAIN

TREASURE MOUNTAIN

Folktales from Southern China
retold by
Catherine Edwards Sadler

ILLUSTRATED BY CHENG MUNG YUN

ATHENEUM   1982   *New York*

CHINESE FOLKTALES were passed down orally through the many generations and collected by folklorists from about 1920 on. There exist many versions of each tale, found in obscure pamphlets, rare folklore weeklies and larger volumes published for the most part after Liberation in 1949. Versions of these tales can be found in the following more accessible collections:

T'ung-hua Yü-yen Hsüan (A Selection of Fairy Tales and Fables) Peking, 1959

Min-chien Wen-hsüeh (Folk Literature) Peking, 1956

Chuang-tsu Min-chien Ku-shih (Folktales of the Chuang People) Peking, 1956

Chung-kuo Min-chien Ku-shih Hsüan (Selections of Chinese Folktales) Peking, 1959

THE AUTHOR would like to thank the following people for their invaluable assistance on this book: Ying Lien of the Foreign Languages Press, Peking; Prof. Bernard Solomon of the Department of Classical and Oriental Languages at Queens College, New York; Mr. Eddie Wang, Ms. Jean Pan and Ms. Grace Ooi of the East Asian Library—Chinese Division of Columbia University, New York, and the general staff of the Harvard-Yenching Institute Library, Harvard University, Boston.

PROPER NAMES in this text have been transcribed in the Wade-Giles system of Romanization.

Library of Congress Cataloging in Publication Data

Sadler, Catherine Edwards.   Treasure mountain.

SUMMARY: A collection of six tales from southern China which reveal the people's sorrows, thoughts, and hopes while passing on age-old customs and beliefs.

1. Tales—China. [1. Folklore—China] I. Cheng, Mung Yun, ill. II. Title.

PZ8.1.S21Tr   398.2'0951   82-1805

ISBN 0-689-30941-4   AACR2

To Alan

CONTENTS

FOREWORD

$\mathcal{M}$AGICAL tools with mysterious pow-
ers, fairies and goblins mingling with the common folk,
great bounty coming to the deserving poor—these are
the themes of the Chinese folktales here. They are folktales, rather than fairy tales, because as their name im-
plies, they have sprung up from the people themselves.
Often tales such as these were the only means of
expression and political dissent available to them in
times of great hardship and oppression. Many were
told by elders to their young to entertain and inspire
hope. Even now folktales are used as a voice of the
people in China to underscore themes current in political thought and to inspire the young to act on these
themes.

The People's Republic of China is the home of some 900 million people. That huge population consists of the Han people, who make up the majority of the population in China, and fifty-three other groups who are China's national minorities. Many of these minorities have languages and cultures of their own.

Since early times there had been great strife between the many minorities and the ruling Han. In fact legend has it that the ancestor of the Han people—said to be the "Yellow Emperor" Huang Ti—battled an alliance of southern tribes as far back as the 27th century B.C. It is believed that he succeeded in pushing back the tribes to the mountain regions and began a policy of open hostility toward the minorities, which lasted the many centuries. Certainly the Han rulers considered the minorities barbarians and denied them even the most basic rights. Hatred of the Han was strong in the hearts of the minority peoples and it surfaces often in their folktales.

The Chuang, T'ung and Yao tribes whose tales are included here shared this hatred for the Han. Many of their folktales, like *Treasure Mountain* and *The Stonemason* portray officials as greedy, evil tyrants. Other tales, such as *The Chuang Brocade* and *Shooting the Moon*, focus on the tribes' own customs and beliefs.

The Han peasant, though not suffering such persecution and oppression, nonetheless suffered many of the minority peoples' hardships. Famine, drought and disease were common visitors to the south and made life for the poor both difficult and threatening. Like Lao Ta in the old Han tale *The Candy Man,* many Han peasants made their living taking menial jobs. However the Han peasant usually accepted the sovereignty of the emperor and his officials as the natural order of Chinese life.

The Magic Brush represents a large body of folktales that have been adapted from ancient tales to reflect the Communist point of view. In ancient texts Ma Liang is given a magic brush with which he paints wondrous objects and riches. Only in newer versions does he reject those riches and confront openly both the landlord and the emperor. Such scenes have been added to show that Ma Liang is the common man fighting against evil and oppression, not interested in self-gain, wanting what is good for his fellow man.

Throughout Chinese folktales, be they of Han or minority origin, ancient or modern, certain themes recur. Time and time again we see the people's desire for a better life free from persecution and oppression, the hope for a good daughter-in-law, a loving, loyal son who will respect and care for the aged, the virtue of humility and kindness over greed and avarice. Each tale was and is a small treasure mountain, providing expression for the common man's sorrows and hopes, teaching the young about age-old customs and beliefs, being a source of amusement, revealing the people's thoughts and hopes for the future.

Today the southern region of China, from which

these six tales come, is a land of great prosperity. Part of this prosperity is due to the great beauty of its mountains, which draws hundreds of thousands of tourists each year. But a large part is due to the Chinese themselves, who have reconciled their cultural differences, united their ideologies and have worked together to bring life back to a once barren land.

TREASURE MOUNTAIN

TREASURE MOUNTAIN

a Yao folktale

*U*NDER the shadow of the great mountain cliffs lived K'o-li and his aged mother. They were very poor and lived in an ancient one-room hut. A terrible famine had swept over their beautiful country and had destroyed their crops of soybeans, wheat and rice.

Each morning K'o-li left his mother and walked in the direction of the rising sun. Soon he would enter the woods where it was said huge tigers prowled. But K'o-li was not afraid. He was certain the celestial beings that lived in the great mountains would protect him from harm.

Each day K'o-li knelt beside the giant Cathaya tree and dug at the earth with his bare hands. His fingers sifted the earth for the roots of the turtle foot plant. All day he dug at the roots. His aged mother would steam the pulp and serve it for supper later. It was not very good and digging the root of the turtle foot plant was hard work, but K'o-li did not mind. He thanked the celestial beings for allowing him to live amidst such great beauty and for creating the turtle foot plant so that he and his mother would not starve.

One day K'o-li went into the forest and knelt under the Cathaya tree as usual. He dug for a very long time but found few roots. At the end of the day when the sun moved toward his hut, he sadly went home.

"Mother, you eat," he insisted that night. "There is little and I am not hungry."

"My child, you eat. You are young and need your strength. Without you I would not be able to survive," his mother replied.

Just then a stooped old man appeared at their door. His whiskers were long and his face was very wrinkled. He looked pale and feeble and leaned heavily against a whittled walking stick.

"Old man, you must be starved," K'o-li's mother cried out. "You look as if you will topple to the earth any moment. Come. Come!"

The old man nodded at her, but he did not speak.

"My child, neither you nor I have wanted to eat

this single portion of food and thus deny the other," the woman said. "Let us go without and give it to the old father."

K'o-li motioned for the old man to enter and quickly handed him the meager fare. The old man ate with relish and in a few minutes the bowl was empty. He then rose and made to leave.

"Old father," K'o-li said, "I have a large basket, which I can strap across my back. You will fit in it. Let me carry you home."

The old man nodded a second time and K'o-li's mother fetched the basket and strapped it onto his back. Then K'o-li bent down and the old man climbed in. K'o-li bowed slowly to his mother and walked outside.

"Which way, father?" he asked his passenger.

The old man pointed a weathered hand toward the peaked mountains that loomed so great in the distance.

They were far away and the old man was not light, but K'o-li kept an even pace as he walked. Once in a while K'o-li wondered about the old man he carried, but most of the time he tried not to think at all. There were dangerously deep gorges to cross and steep mountains to climb and they demanded attention. The old man never uttered a word and K'o-li never slowed down. It was morning by the time they reached the large stone cave in which the old man lived. K'o-li was tired and glad to have reached his destination at last.

He bent down so that the old man could climb out of the basket. Just then a lovely girl with skin the color of milk and hair black as a moonless night appeared.

"Grandfather!" she cried out. "You have come. I thought you were either lost or dead!"

The old man smiled broadly and finally spoke. "My granddaughter, Mi-mi, this young man gave his food to me and carried me on his back a great distance. Take off your earrings and turn them into magical keys so that he may open the mountains."

The maiden Mi-mi bowed to her grandfather and quickly took a golden earring from her left ear and a silver one from her right. Then she knelt beside a large rock and began to hammer out two keys—one of gold and the other of silver.

"Young man," she said to K'o-li when she was done, "on the right side of this cliff is Treasure Mountain and in it is a huge stone cave. You will see a yellow stone just like a door at its entrance. Put the golden key into the tiny hole in the stone and it will open. Within, you will find countless treasures. Take what you will. The stone door will have closed on its own after you have entered the cave. When you wish to leave, open it with the silver key by placing it into the hole at the back of the door. Take care not to lose this key or you will be shut in the cave forever!"

"But I cannot take your beautiful earrings!" K'o-li exclaimed in dismay.

"Hurry! Go now!" the old man shouted in a voice

that seemed to have no origin. "A tiger is coming and will eat you. Go now!"

K'o-li quickly looked in all directions but he could find no sign of the tiger. At that moment the old father and the maiden disappeared into the cave. A large stone door dropped down, sealing it off. K'o-li was quite alone. A pair of shimmering keys lay at his feet. He picked them up and looked at them. Their brightness was dazzling and reminded K'o-li of the sun beaming down on his favorite river, the Likiang. He waited for the old father and his granddaughter to return but they did not and so he went home.

K'o-li told his mother of the maiden's words and showed her the beautiful keys. She listened solemnly until he had finished his story.

"My child, we dig turtle foot roots to eat a little pulp. It is a great honor that they have entrusted you with these keys. I do not think we are betraying that trust to want a little more from life. Perhaps there are tools hidden within the cave that will help us bring the land back to life."

K'o-li thought of the turtle foot roots he dug each day with his bare hands. It could not be wrong to want to work with tools instead. And so K'o-li took the keys and walked all the way to Treasure Mountain. And there he discovered the yellow stone door. K'o-li took the golden key from his sleeve and placed it into the lock. The door began to open.

K'o-li checked the silver key in his sleeve and cautiously entered the cave. Suddenly there was a large noise. It was the yellow door slamming shut.

The cave seemed to jump and dance with light. Before K'o-li lay a mound of treasure. Objects of gold and silver and wondrous strands of pearls met his gaze. He stood very still, not knowing what to do. The shimmering beauty of the treasure blinded and confused him. But then he thought of the turtle foot plant and his dear mother and he remembered why he had come. A white stone grinder lay in the corner of the cave.

"I'll take this home and earn my living grinding. That will be good," he thought contentedly as he took up the tool. Then he walked back to the door, opened it with the silver key and left. Behind him the great door slammed shut. K'o-li happily walked the long distance home.

His aged mother was very pleased with her son and placed the white grinder in the middle of the room. Then she walked over to it and tried to turn its lid to see how it worked. Suddenly small nuggets of something yellow began to spill out. They were beans. Thousands and thousands of soybeans. The more they turned the lid the more the room was filled with golden soybeans. They could scarcely believe their eyes! So full did the room become that mother and son soon began to slip and slide. And the sight was so strange and funny that they began to laugh. They laughed and laughed till their bodies ached and their heads felt light. They had not laughed for some time and it felt good.

"How can we possibly use all these beans? There are too many for us. We must give some to our neighbors," K'o-li said as he wiped a laughter tear from his eye. And so he filled his basket with soybeans and paid a visit to all the people of the region. And each day that the grinder produced the creamy-colored beans, K'o-li took up his basket and set out to visit his neighbors.

Now, such a miracle as this could scarcely be kept secret. It was not long before word of it spread along the rivers and over the mountains and the king came to hear of it. He immediately sent a high official with a small band of soldiers to K'o-li's ancient hut. They pushed him down and stole off with the grinder. At the palace the king strutted and crowed like a peacock in love. He gazed at his new treasure in delight. But when he went to fondle it, the grinder turned to dust. The king was very displeased. "Behead the useless official who brought me this grinder!" he screamed, his face blowing up to look like the full moon.

"MY SON, do you still have the keys to the great yellow door?" the aged woman asked her son when she heard that the grinder had been stolen by the king's men.

"Yes, I have carried them both with me each day."

"Then return to Treasure Mountain. Surely it is not wrong to take another tool with which to feed the people of Kwangsi."

K'o-li walked back to Treasure Mountain. He opened the large yellow stone door with the golden key. He was blinded once again by the startling beauty within. But in time he grew used to the brilliance of its sheen and could see that a yellow stone mortar lay to one side. He took it into his arms and returned home.

As soon as K'o-li was again in his ancient hut, he and his mother began to pound at the mortar with an old wooden pestle. No sooner had the pestle touched the mortar than pearls of white rice began to tumble out. The more they pounded, the more the rice piled into the room. And soon the good son could scarcely see his mother for the rice. It was as if the world had turned and it had finally snowed in Kwangsi. K'o-li and his mother laughed and laughed, so comical was its sight. And the next day he gathered up the rice into his basket and joyfully spread his bounty with one and all.

But word travels quickly and it was not long before the king came to hear of the mortar. Again he ordered a high official to fetch the prize, only this time he sent a larger troop of soldiers. The soldiers stormed the little hut, knocking over the table and three chairs and K'o-li's aged mother.

In the palace the king paced in front of the mortar like a caged tiger contemplating his escape. He had to be very careful how he touched that mortar. He did not want it to crumble before his eyes. Very gently, ever so carefully, he touched the rim of the tool. But the mortar instantly turned to powdered clay. The king fumed and spat till his face turned the color of the sunset after a humid day. Then he yelled, "Behead the useless official who brought me this mortar," and collapsed in rage.

K'O-LI went again to Treasure Mountain and brought back a hoe with which to till the land. He carefully weeded the earth in front of his hut and began to pull the hoe across the dirt, when suddenly what did he see but great stalks growing out of the barren land! He touched the hoe to the earth and stalk after stalk of honey-colored wheat shot straight up. He cried for his mother but could not see her when she came, so high were the mighty stalks. But each laughed in delight to see how the earth had come alive again. And in the morning K'o-li filled his basket with the golden grain and distributed it far and near.

Of course, the king came to hear of the magic hoe, but he would not be fooled again. "Bring me this young man, K'o-li," he shouted to his last high official and his biggest army. It was not long before the hills of Kwangsi were thick with soldiers who descended on the small ancient hut, nearly knocking it down. They bound K'o-li hand and foot and carried him off to the palace. They brought him before the king, who sat on a huge, ornate throne with the sun and the stars embossed upon it. On either side of the king stood executioners. They were dressed in dark robes with shining axes and knives in their huge, scarred hands.

"From where do your great treasures come?" the

king demanded. "Speak or I shall behead you as I have my high officials!"

K'o-li thought for a while. Finally he said, "All right, I will tell you. My treasures come from deep in the mountains. There is great treasure there. It is endless and I have the golden key that unlocks it all."

The king laughed and rocked with delight. He twisted his long, thin mustache in pleasure. "Good, good," he cried, "I am glad you have seen reason. Give me that key. We shall go there at once. You will be my guide. Men! Bring me my sedan!"

A sedan chair, embroidered with golden threads, was brought to the king. He climbed aboard and within an hour the king, K'o-li and the king's entire army were marching toward Treasure Mountain. They did not stop until the great yellow door was before them. The king awkwardly climbed out of his chair and, trembling with excitement, fit the golden key into the door. The door opened and the king and his men rushed into the cave. Behind him the great door shut tight.

K'o-li shouted from without: "King, you would deceive your people and rob them of their only food in a time of famine. The silver key that lets you out is in my hand. You are locked within forever. May you enjoy your treasure!"

K'o-li returned home in a very good state of mind. The next day he tilled the land with his magic hoe and visited his neighbors as usual. But then he remembered

the maiden with skin like milk and the beautiful earrings he had taken from her.

"I have lost one of the maiden's earrings. What
shall I do?" he asked his mother in dismay.

"We shall go to her and explain what has passed.
We will apologize for the key's loss and bow before her
in shame. That is all that we can do."

Mother and son filled two baskets with soybeans,
wheat and rice and carried them through the woods,
over the deep gorges, and onto the steep mountain
slopes. Finally they saw the old father and his lovely
granddaughter sitting peacefully at the entrance to their
cave.

K'o-li bowed deeply to them and lowered his eyes.
"I am sorry the golden key is lost," he said softly, hand-
ing the maiden the silver key. She smiled, took it in her
hand and swiftly turned it back into an earring.

K'o-li's mother turned to the old man. "Father,
here are two baskets filled with soybeans, wheat and
rice. They are not much more than a sampling, but we
could carry no more. They come from the precious tools
K'o-li took from Treasure Mountain."

"Old woman, I do not need your food. Better you
keep it and give it to your neighbors as you have in the
past. But my granddaughter needs an honest husband
and I can think of no better than your K'o-li." He then
turned and walked into his cave. Behind him the stone
door suddenly dropped shut. The maiden Mi-mi was
left behind.

14

The old woman took the hands of her new daughter-in-law and her good son K'o-li and together they walked back to their ancient hut deep in the region of Kwangsi, where to this day the crops abound like nowhere else on earth.

And it is said that if you venture deep into the mountains you will come upon a great stone door. And beyond that door there is great wealth and treasure. But it will remain hidden till there are no stars in the sky or days in the year, for no one has the key.

THE CHUANG BROCADE

a Chuang folktale

*I*N a valley at the bottom of a high mountain there once lived a Tan-pu, as old Chuang women are called. She lived in a small, tumbledown wood hut with her three sons named Le-me, Le-tui-e and Le-je.

The Tan-pu's people were famous for their weaving since ancient times, especially for the patterned cloth known as Chuang brocade. There were many good weavers in the Tan-pu's time, but none were as skilled as she. Her work was renowned for its beauty. Her scenes were so colorful and intricate that they looked just like paintings. So good was her work that, despite famine and drought, the Tan-pu could always sell her weaving. And she and her three sons were always able to live on the money she made from her beautiful Chuang brocade.

Then one day the Tan-pu went to town to buy rice. On the way she passed a small shop in which hung a striking painting. The Tan-pu could not resist going in to have a closer look. The painting was of an ideal estate. Tall, strong buildings stood in the foreground. An orchard filled with colorful fruit spread beyond the main house. To one side was a lovely garden with a fish pond and fragrant flowers of every description. Chickens and ducks scampered through the courtyard. Cattle and sheep grazed lazily in the distant fields.

The Tan-pu had never seen such a place as this. She thought of the one-room hut in which she had always lived; she thought of the dry land her dead husband had never been able to till; of her poor eyesight from years of weaving intricate patterns in her Chuang brocade. How she longed to live on such an estate! How she longed to eat fruit and vegetables with every meal. The Tan-pu could not take her eyes off the painting. It filled her very being with peace and happiness. And so the old woman took out her rice money and bought the painting.

"Wouldn't it be wonderful if we could live in such a wonderful place, Le-me?" the Tan-pu said to her eldest son that night.

17

Le-me looked sharply at his mother and said, "Such thoughts are but dreams. You waste your time thinking of such things."

"If only we could live in such a place, Le-tui-e," she said to her second son.

"Only in the next world," Le-tui-e answered somberly.

"Le-je, I swear I shall die of disappointment if I cannot live in that ideal estate," she told her youngest son. Then the old woman gazed sadly at her painting and let out a deep, melancholy sigh.

Le-je was very quiet for some time. But finally he looked at his mother and told her, "The patterns you create in your Chuang brocade are so lifelike, why do you not weave an estate just like the one in this painting. Weaving it will be nearly as good as if you were really living in such a place."

The Tan-pu meditated on what her youngest son had said. Then she smacked her lips and said cheerfully, "You are right, my son. I must weave a brocade of the ideal estate. Otherwise I will surely die of disappointment!"

So the very next day the Tan-pu went to town and bought herself the finest silk yarn. And the moment she was at home again she sat down at her loom and began to weave.

From then on the Tan-pu wove every morning and every afternoon. She wove every evening and every night. Days soon turned to months and still the old woman wove. She wove so long her sons had to use their small savings to buy food. In time, when the savings was gone, they had to go out and chop wood for money.

"You weave all day, but never sell anything," complained Le-me and Le-tui-e. "You live on the rice we buy with the money we get from chopping wood. But we are tired and do not want to chop wood any more."

But the Tan-pu did not reply. She did not even look up from her Chuang brocade.

"Leave our mother alone," said Le-je to his older brothers. "Let her weave her beautiful estate. Otherwise she will never be content. Do you want our mother to die of disappointment? I will chop the wood for you."

And so from then on Le-je chopped the wood for the entire family, and he worked day and night while his mother wove her Chuang brocade.

At night the Tan-pu burned pine branches for light. They smoked so much that her eyes became red and bloodshot, but still she did not stop. She wove her cloth until her eyes smarted and tears dropped onto the brocade. But even then she did not stop. Instead, she wove her tears into long rivers and small ponds.

For three years the Tan-pu wove her fabric until finally she had created her beautiful estate. How wonderful was that piece of Chuang brocade! How lifelike were the grounds, the gardens, the orchards. One could almost smell the flowers in bloom, one could almost taste the orchard's colorful fruit. All three of the Tan-pu's sons gazed in admiration at their mother's work. It was the most beautiful piece of Chuang brocade they had ever seen.

The Tan-pu stretched her stiff old body and rubbed her tired, bloodshot eyes. Her face beamed in joy as she looked at that piece of brocade. Its beauty made her so happy that she suddenly began to laugh.

Then a great gust of wind came from the east and lifted the Tan-pu's Chuang brocade. In a moment the wind had carried the cloth out of the hut, high into the sky and far, far away to the east.

The Tan-pu cried out and ran after her brocade. She ran until she fainted. Her sons had to carry her back to their hut where they laid her on her bed. And when she awoke she told her eldest son:

"Le-me, go to the east and find me my Chuang brocade. I have woven it for three years. Day and night I have lived in it. Now it means more to me than life itself. I shall surely die if I do not get it back!"

So Le-me went to the east. After a month he came to a mountain pass where a stone horse stood. Its mouth was open as though it yearned to eat the red berries that grew near. A stone house stood close by and on its stoop sat a fat old woman.

"Where are you going, my son?" she asked Le-me.

"I am looking for a piece of Chuang brocade," the Tan-pu's eldest son replied. "My mother has spent three years weaving it. A great gust of wind came and took it to the east."

"The brocade was carried off by the fairies of Sun Mountain," said the fat old woman. "They want to copy it as it is so well made. But it is very difficult to reach Sun Mountain where the fairies live. First you must knock out two of your teeth and place them in the mouth of my stone horse. Then he will move his mouth and eat ten of the red berries. When he has eaten the berries, you must mount him. He will then take you to the east. But you will have to pass through Flame Mountain where giant flames will lash out at you. You must huddle close to your horse and tightly clench your teeth. You must not utter a single word. For if you utter one word you will be burned to ashes! After passing through Flame Mountain you will come to the Icy Sea. The waves of the sea are filled with sharp ice that can cut and bruise you. Again you must huddle close to the horse and clench your teeth. You must not shiver. If you shiver at all from the cold, you will fall to the very bottom of the Icy Sea! When you have crossed both Flame Mountain and the Icy Sea, you will finally see Sun Mountain and be able to bring back your mother's Chuang brocade."

Now Le-me was not a brave fellow and he thought in fear of the pain from knocking out his teeth and the burning heat of Flame Mountain and the freezing cold of the Icy Sea. His fear turned his face as pale as the whitest ghost. So the old woman said to him:

"I see you cannot endure such pain, even for your mother's sake. Then do not go. I will give you an iron box filled with gold and you can return to the south a wealthy man."

So Le-me took the iron box filled with gold and started for home. But he had not gone far before he realized his gold would go farther if he did not have to share it with his family. And so Le-me turned to the north.

For two months the Tan-pu waited for her eldest son. Each day she went to the door and looked for him. But when he did not return she said to her second son, Le-tui-e:

"Go to the east, find out what happened to your brother, and bring me back my Chuang brocade."

And so Le-tui-e also went to the east where he met the old fat woman sitting on her stoop. And she told him what had happened to Le-me and how he could get the Chuang brocade. And he too turned pale as a ghost when he thought of the pain and the heat and the cold. And so he too took the iron box filled with gold. And he also turned to the north rather than share his fortune with his family.

And the Tan-pu waited another two months. Each day she looked out the door and wept for lost sons and her lost brocade. And with each passing day her eyes grew dimmer, until she could hardly see.

Then Le-je, the youngest son, said to his mother:

"Perhaps my brothers have met some danger and

cannot get home. Let me go to the east. I will look for them and bring you back your Chuang brocade."

So Le-je went to the east as had his older brothers. And eventually he came to the same mountain pass where the old woman sat. She told him what had happened to his brothers and how he could find the Chuang brocade.

"I will not go after my brothers," said the Tan-pu's youngest son, "for they doubt the importance of the brocade. But I know my mother will die if it is not returned." With that he bent down, picked up a stone, knocked out two teeth and put them into the horse's mouth. Suddenly the stone horse's mouth began to move, and he was able to eat the ten red berries. Le-je mounted the horse and in moments they were traveling toward the east.

In three days they reached Flame Mountain. It was as red as the freshest blood and hotter than seven suns. Le-je huddled close to his horse, clenched his teeth, and, hot as the mountain was, he did not utter a single word.

Horse and rider rode through Flame Mountain for an entire day. By the time they reached the other side, Le-je's skin was shriveled and burned, but still he remained silent and still he huddled close to his horse. They had only been out of the mountain a short time when a freezing cold pierced Le-je to the bone. Great sheets of ice lashed out at him as he passed over the frozen waters of the Icy Sea. The cold stung and bruised

7

his body, but Le-je held tight to his horse, and in time he could see the golden rays of Sun Mountain. Girlish singing and laughter rang out from a mansion high on the mountain. Le-je knew then that the dangers of the east were now behind him and the end of his quest was near.

He rode up to the mansion, dismounted and walked into the great hall. Hundreds of fairies sat at looms, busily weaving brocade. In the middle of the hall hung the most beautiful cloth of all. It was his mother's Chuang brocade.

The fairies stopped work on seeing the young man. Le-je told them how his mother was pining for her brocade, and how he feared she would die if she did not get it back.

"Very well," said one of the fairies. "We will work through the night to finish. Tomorrow you can return to the south with your mother's brocade."

Then the fairies hung a shining pearl on the ceiling of the great hall, and they worked through the night by its luminous light.

The first to finish was a beautiful fairy dressed all in red. When she compared her work with the Tan-pu's brocade she saw that, though she had worked hard, it was not as well made.

"Wouldn't it be wonderful to live in the Tan-pu's Chuang brocade?" the red fairy thought to herself. "It is more beautiful than our mansion here on Sun Mountain."

And so while the others were still busy with their weaving, the red fairy took a red silk thread and embroidered the image of herself on the Tan-pu's Chuang brocade.

When all the fairies had finished their weaving and had left the hall to rest, Le-je rolled up the brocade and placed it in his blouse, close to his heart. Then he left the mansion of the fairies of Sun Mountain, mounted his horse and traveled toward the west. He huddled close to his horse and clenched his teeth as he passed through the Icy Sea and Flame Mountain. But the cold and the heat did not bother him, for close to his breast he carried the Tan-pu's precious brocade.

When he reached the fat old woman sitting on her stoop, she asked him to dismount, took the two teeth from her horse's mouth and placed them back into Le-je's. Instantly the horse turned to stone. Then the woman brought out a pair of deerskin slippers, which she asked Le-je to put on.

"With these slippers you will be able to return home quickly," she told Le-je. "And this you must do, for your mother has turned blind and is soon to die."

So Le-je put on the slippers, bowed low to the old woman and in minutes was standing again in his family hut. His mother lay on her bed, looking so thin and pale that indeed Le-je thought she was about to die.

"Mother! Mother!" he cried out. "Please do not die. I have found your Chuang brocade. The fairies of Sun Mountain took it to copy because it was so well made!" Le-je took the brocade from his blouse and spread it before her. It gleamed so brightly that the Tan-pu's sight came back to her. Color returned to her face and strength to her old bones. "Oh my youngest son!" she said. "It is too dark in here. Let us take the brocade into the sunlight!"

The old mother and her son went outside and spread the Chuang brocade lovingly on the ground. A breeze rose up from the east and drew the brocade out —making it bigger and bigger—until it covered as much land as the eye could see at one time.

Suddenly their little hut was gone. In its place were tall, strong buildings. Around them was a green garden, a fruit-filled orchard, golden fields—all exactly as the Tan-pu had woven them into her Chuang brocade! And by the fish pond stood a lovely maiden all dressed in red. It was the red fairy who had embroidered herself into the Tan-pu's brocade.

The Tan-pu and her good son took hold of each other's hand and walked into the garden. The Tan-pu welcomed the maiden who preferred to live on the estate than remain a fairy on Sun Mountain, and in time the son took her for his wife. When neighbors came to visit the Tan-pu's hut and saw a grand estate in its place, they were invited in to share its great bounty.

But there were some who could not see it at all, perhaps because they could not believe that fairy tales can come true.

In time Le-me and Le-tui-e spent the gold that was

in the fat old woman's iron boxes and so, not wanting to work for a living, they finally went home. But look as they may, neither could find a trace of their brother, their mother, the old tumbledown wood hut or the Tan-pu's beautiful Chuang brocade.

THE CANDY MAN

---

a Han folktale

*T*HERE were once two brothers who were as different as two brothers could be. One was greedy while the other was humble. One was jealous while the other was generous. The greedy brother was named Lao Ta and his good younger brother was named Lao Erh.

When Lao Ta, and Lao Erh's father died, Lao Ta seized the family property. He rented out the land for a huge sum of money and became a very rich man. But his younger brother, Lao Erh, did not complain and continued to take odd jobs to eke out a meager living.

Then one day the younger brother, Lao Erh, was hired to deliver two buckets of syrup to a merchant on the other side of the mountain. Lao Erh hung the buckets at either end of a long stick, balanced it on his shoulder, and started up the mountain. He had just reached midway when it began to rain. The path became slippery and Lao Erh lost his balance. He fell and rolled all the way to the bottom of the mountain, buckets of syrup and all.

There lay Lao Erh, covered in sticky syrup! Just as he was about to get up, seven goblins walked by.

"Why, it is an enormous candy man!" they cried delightedly, and began to eat the sugared syrup right off his body—for as everyone knows, goblins love to eat sweets.

"Let's take the candy home and eat it there!" a second goblin said. All the goblins nodded furiously in agreement. Together they carried poor sugar-coated Lao Erh to their cave deep in the mountain.

The goblins placed their candy man on a stone table and crowded all around, ready for their second helping.

One goblin with a long horn growing straight out of his head said to a smaller goblin, "Go fetch the treasure so that we can get on with the meal! Then we'll go down the mountain and conjure up all sorts of fun!"

So the little goblin ran to a dark corner of the cave and brought out a tiny drum. The long-horned goblin beat on the tiny drum and instantly the cave was filled with the delicious smell of cooked food. Lao Erh, meanwhile, had not eaten in some time and the aroma was making him very hungry. But he knew from legends that goblins ate at least one human a year, and he did not want to find out whether they had already eaten this year's share. So he lay very still and watched to see where they put their tiny magic drum.

After the goblins had eaten their meal and nibbled on Lao Erh's sugar coating, they left the cave. As soon as they were gone, Lao Erh jumped off the table, took the magic drum, hid it inside his coat, and ran all the way home with his heart pounding in fear. But from then on Lao Erh did not have to worry where his next meal would come from.

Lao Erh's older brother, Lao Ta, of course came to hear of the tiny magic drum. And true to his nature, he was beside himself with jealousy over his brother's good fortune. And so he took two buckets of syrup and carried them up the mountain just as his brother had a few days before. Halfway up he forced himself to slip, for it had not rained again. He rolled all the way down the mountain, buckets of syrup and all. There he lay, all covered in syrup, waiting for the goblins to appear. And sure enough, they did. When they saw Lao Ta they were very excited and shouted to each other in high, squeaky voices:

"Look! Look! Here's that enormous candy! And we thought we had lost it! Quick, let us take it back to the cave."

And the goblins carried Lao Ta back to their cave deep in the mountains. Lao Ta was very pleased with himself and wondered what magical object would soon be his.

But when they put Lao Ta on the stone table, the long-horned goblin said, "Last time that candy man got away with our tiny magic drum. We had better boil it up and make ourselves sweet drinks. Then we can safely take out our treasure for dinner."

All the little goblins enthusiastically shouted their agreement. They put Lao Ta into a big cooking pot and filled it up with water. Then they lit the fire. It was not long before the water became uncomfortably hot and Lao Ta began to cook. He jumped straight out of the cooking pot and bolted for the door. The littlest goblin shrieked out: "Our candy! Our enormous candy man! It's running away! Catch it quick!" And out ran all seven goblins after Lao Ta.

He ran as fast as his sticky, steamy legs would carry him, but the goblins were faster. They caught their candy and brought it back to the cave.

"Here we thought it was an enormous candy figure, when it was really a man!" shouted a goblin.

"Let us punish the cheat!" shouted a second.

"Let's not eat or kill him, but rather give him something to always remember us by," said a third chuckling. And he grabbed hold of Lao Ta's nose and began to pull it with all his might. He pulled so hard that it stretched right out. The other goblins hooted and cheered and merrily grabbed hold of it and pulled it in turn. When they were all done, Lao Ta's nose was seven feet long! The goblins were very pleased with this and cheerfully kicked the imposter out.

Lao Ta gathered up his long nose and slowly made his way home. By the time he arrived, his arms were aching from carrying the weight of his nose. He called out for his wife and she rushed to greet her husband, expecting him to have brought back a magic object from the goblins' cave. She had just stepped into the room when her husband let out a painful scream.

"You are standing on my nose!" he cried.

"What!?" replied his confused wife, "how can that be?" Then she stepped back and took a good look at her husband. Sure enough, his nose was so long it hung to the ground.

As he told her what happened, Lao Ta mopped his brow and whimpered miserably. When his sad story was over, his wife sighed deeply and said, "There must be a way to correct this. Goblins can cure what they have caused. All tales say so. Perhaps we can send Lao Erh back to the goblin cave and he can find out what must be done." So saying, she ran straight off to find her brother-in-law, Lao Erh.

Now, Lao Erh had discovered that his magic drum had many uses. Not only did it produce food! It could grant one any wish. Lao Erh was not a greedy man, and he had no desire to sit home idly, so he asked the

drum for some money and bought tools to work his land. Then he locked away his tiny magic drum.

He was working in the fields when his sister-in-law ran up and told Lao Erh what had happened. "The goblins have pulled Lao Ta's nose!" she cried. "It is so long that he has to wrap it around his hand, otherwise it would drag along the ground. The pain from the weight is terrible. Oh, please, can you return to the goblin's cave and find out how to make it small once more?"

So good Lao Erh, even though his brother had cheated him of their father's land, went back to the mountain. He found the goblins' cave without trouble. Hearing no sounds, he went inside and waited behind the door for the goblins to return.

"I smell a stranger!" a goblin shouted on entering.

"I smell a man!" shouted another.

"We must make sure no one is trying to steal our treasure!" shouted yet a third.

The goblins ran frantically in all directions, looking for an intruder. But although they made a great deal of noise, they did not find Lao Erh.

Finally they sat down around their stone table. The littlest goblin ran to a dark spot and brought out a tiny copper gong. The long-horned goblin beat it three times and instantly a banquet appeared.

"We must take good care of this gong," he said. "It is all that is left of our treasure." And he hung it about his neck.

"What fun it was to stretch that candy man's nose yesterday," one of the goblins said during the meal. "I am sure he came to steal our gong. He'll never dare come here again!"

"And so he'll never learn the cure!" agreed another. "How could he know to rap the tiny magic drum and shout 'Shrink!' "

"Yes, with each rap his nose would get shorter! But he'll never find that out!" And all the goblins laughed heartily to think that the candy man would always have such a long nose.

After dinner the little goblins left their cave to find some mischief. Lao Erh waited until their merry voices grew dim. Then he crept out from behind the door and ran all the way home.

Once there, he fetched his tiny magic drum and ran to his brother's house. He immediately told Lao Ta and his wife about the cure.

"Hurry!" shouted his sister-in-law. "Make his nose small again. He is dying of the pain!"

So Lao Erh rapped on the tiny drum and shouted, "Shrink!" Instantly his brother's nose shortened a few inches. Lao Erh rapped on the tiny drum a second time and shouted, "Shrink," again. The nose shortened a few inches more. He rapped on the drum and shouted "Shrink!" a third time, and his brother's nose shortened some more. But Lao Ta's wife was impatient, for her husband's nose was still very long and heavy.

"It will take you forever to cure him at that pace!"

37

she shouted at Lao Erh. "Give me that drum!" And she grabbed the tiny magic drum right out of Lao Erh's hand. She began to rap furiously on it, yelling "Shrink! Shrink! Shrink!" With each rap and shout Lao Ta's nose grew shorter and shorter. But his wife persisted, banging on the drum and shouting, "Shrink! Shrink! Shrink!" until finally she struck the drum so hard that it shattered into thousands of tiny pieces.

And from then on, the greedy Lao Ta had no nose at all.

SHOOTING THE MOON

a Yao folktale

*L*ONG ago, in ancient times, there was no moon nor any stars. The sun alone dominated the sky and when it set for the night, the world was wrapped in utter darkness.

Then, suddenly, a fiery moon appeared in the sky. It had sharp edges and corners and was hotter than any sun. So fierce were its rays that it scorched the crops and burned the people below.

And there was little anyone could do. Long into the night the suffering folk mopped their brows and tossed miserably in their beds.

There lived at that time a young married couple. The man was called Ya La and he was a fine archer. Each day he climbed to the top of the mountain to hunt. His wife was called Ni Wo and she spent her day embroidering fine cloth.

Now Ni Wo was a good woman and she cared greatly for her people. So one day she told her husband, "This moon is too hot for mankind. We cannot stand by and let it cause such suffering. You are the best archer in the region, surely you can shoot down this wretched moon."

So Ya La took up his bow and arrow and climbed back up to the top of the mountain. There he took a deep, determined breath, pulled back his bowstring as far as it would bear and shot an arrow at that fiery moon. The arrow sailed high up into the sky directly toward the moon, but it did not reach its mark. Halfway it turned and began to fall back to earth. Ya La shot arrow after arrow at the fiery moon, but try as he might his arrows always fell short. Ya La remained at the mountaintop until his last arrow was shot. Then he looked sorrowfully at the moon above that was causing his people so much pain. He knew his hollow-cheeked people could not survive its poisonous rays for long. But the archer Ya La did not know what to do.

At that very moment there came a cracking sound from behind him. Turning round, he found himself face to face with a weathered, worn-looking old man. The man bowed to Ya La and began to speak:

"Deep in the southern mountain there lives the strong tiger. You must eat its flesh if you wish your arrows to reach the moon. You must make its tail your bow and his tendon your bowstring. In the northern mountain there lives a tall deer; you must use the tip of his antler for your arrow. Then shoot the fiery moon till it spins."

The archer bowed to the old man in return and went home. He told his wife of his strange meeting and the words the old man had said. Then they spoke of how they could capture the strong tiger and the tall deer.

"You are a fine archer, Ya La," Ni Wo said. "Can you not shoot them with your bow and arrow."

"I have often tried," Ya La replied. "But the tiger's hide is thick and the deer is quick. No, I must use a net to catch the strong tiger and the tall deer."

So Ni Wo cut her own hair for her husband's net. And as her hair fell to the ground, new hair grew back in its place. Then the good wife wove her hair into an enormous net. She worked for thirty days and thirty nights, until at last she was satisfied that it was strong enough to capture the tiger and the deer. Then husband and wife went to the southern mountain.

The journey was long and hard-going and the couple often had to climb high cliffs and wade through ravines, but they encouraged each other until at last they reached the tiger's den. There they placed Ni Wo's net. It was not very long before the huge beast stepped out of his den in search of food. In an instant he was caught up in the net and struggling for his freedom. His cries could be heard over the mountains and through the valleys, but Ni Wo's net was strong. Then the archer and his wife killed the tiger and dragged him home. But they did not remain for long. They gathered up their net and started for the northern mountain. They had to travel over dried lakes and through dense forests, but they plodded on until at last they reached their destination. There they set their net and waited for the tall deer. In time they caught the deer and tightened their net about him. He butted it with his strong, sharp horns, but Ni Wo's net was well made and it did not rip. And so the brave couple killed the tall deer and dragged it home as well.

Then Ni Wo prepared a meal of the tiger's flesh and Ya La ate. Soon his strength increased so that he could twist metal with his bare hands. He made a bow with the tiger's tail and a bowstring with the tiger's tendon. He shaped an arrow from the tall deer's horn and climbed once again to the mountaintop.

Ya La looked up at the blazing fiery moon. Then he pulled back the tendon bowstring. The deer-horn arrow sailed up—higher and higher—until it reached the moon. Suddenly there was a great noise. Sparks lit up the sky. The arrow bounded back to earth where Ya La placed it again in his bow. Over and over he shot the arrow and each time it hit the moon, an edge or a corner broke off and the pieces scattered across the sky. A hundred times Ya La shot the single arrow. And when he was done the moon was round and smooth and spinning like a top. And throughout the sky were shining stars, each formed from a fragment of the fiery moon. But still the moon was hot—still it scorched the fields and burned the people. So Ya La went home with his head hung low.

"Ni Wo," he said sadly to his wife. "I no longer know what to do. The moon is as hot as ever. If only we could somehow cover up its poisonous rays."

Now at that moment Ni Wo was working on a lovely embroidery. It was a picture of an ideal garden with a tall Cassia tree, under which sat the image of Ni Wo. A little hut, much like her own, stood to the side. And in the meadow in the distance cows and sheep lazily grazed. She was just about to embroider the image of her husband herding the flock when he came home.

"Take this embroidery and tie it to your arrow-head," she said at once. "Then shoot it up at the moon. Perhaps it will cover the moon and curtain its fiery heat."

So Ya La took his wife's embroidery and went once more to the mountaintop. And there he strung his bow and shot his deer-horn arrow. Higher and higher it rose until it reached the fiery moon. Ni Wo's embroidery unwrapped and spread smoothly across the moon. The

43

air suddenly became cool and pleasant. And Ya La could hear the sound of his people's laughter and merriment as they danced at the base of the mountain.

He remained for some time at the mountaintop admiring the new cool moon. There were shapes and forms across its surface, but at first he paid them little attention. Then, suddenly, they seemed to move. He strained his eyes to make out the forms . . . surely, that was his own wife's image upon the moon! And it seemed to be beckoning to him!

Meanwhile, Ni Wo was standing in front of her door admiring her husband's work when she too saw the image on the moon. No sooner had she seen it than she began to rise up—higher and higher—until at last she reached the moon and merged with her own image.

Ya La watched in despair as his dear wife sailed up through the sky to the new moon. He shouted wildly:

"Ni Wo, Ni Wo, my beloved wife. Do not leave me! Why did you not embroider me into your cloth? Oh, Ni Wo, I cannot live without you. Please, please come back!"

But Ni Wo could not come back. She cried out and pulled at her hair in torment. As she did her hair became longer and longer. She braided it and when the moon spun around and faced the mountaintop she dipped it down toward her Ya La. He desperately stretched out his hands and just caught hold of the end of his wife's braid. Then he scaled up it—higher and higher—until at last he was in the arms of his dear wife, Ni Wo.

And if you look up at the cool moon you will see them there, the archer and his wife. Sometimes she is sitting under the Cassia tree while Ya La herds their flock. But other times they are standing arm in arm, gazing out at the thousands of glittering stars that once —long, long ago—belonged to a fiery moon.

THE MAGIC BRUSH

a Han folktale

DEEP in the mountains, high above the little village of Clear Glade, lived an orphan boy named Ma Liang. Ma Liang was all alone in the world, for his parents were both dead. But Ma Liang was strong as the water buffalo and brave as the prowling tiger and he feared little. Many villagers had warned him about the strange spirits who made their home in Feather Mountain where he lived. They told him time and time again to move to Clear Glade where he would be safe. But Ma Liang loved Feather Mountain and was sure that if indeed spirits lived in Feather Mountain they were both good and kind.

Each day Ma Liang left his small cave in the mountainside to gather firewood and cut reeds along the river that flowed at the base of Feather Mountain. Every afternoon he dragged his bundle down from the mountain and into the village where he sold the wood and reeds at market. They brought him but a few pennies, but Ma Liang lived simply and he did not need or want much.

After his work was done, Ma Liang returned to Feather Mountain. He loved to sit by the riverbank and watch the shimmering fish as they darted and dodged through the water. He loved to watch the setting sun as it made its way over Clear Glade. Most of all, he loved to study the birds and animals that also lived on Feather Mountain. Their shapes and beauty fascinated Ma Liang and he often wished that he could learn to paint. But Ma Liang had no brush.

One day Ma Liang was walking by a private school where the sons of wealthy landlords studied. Through the window he could see the figure of the schoolmaster as he leaned over a low table. He held a long, fine paintbrush in his hand. Ma Liang walked closer. He could not take his eyes off the paintbrush. Each stroke drew him closer and closer to the room. Before he knew it, Ma Liang had climbed through the window and was standing within feet of the beautiful brush.

49

"I want to learn to paint," said Ma Liang to the schoolmaster. "I want to paint the beauty I see on Feather Mountain. But I cannot afford a paintbrush. Please, will you lend me one? I am sure you have many here. I promise to return it shortly."

"What!" exclaimed the schoolmaster, whose hair was the color of freshly fallen snow. "A little beggar wants to paint! Painting is for scholars not for little beggars such as you. You are daydreaming to think you can learn to paint!" The master shook his thick beautiful brush at Ma Liang and chased the orphan boy away.

Ma Liang returned sadly to his cave in Feather Mountain. "Why shouldn't I learn to paint?" he asked himself that evening. "What difference does it make that I am poor? I can see as clearly as the most learned scholar!"

With that Ma Liang decided to learn to paint without a brush. And so from then on when he went to the top of the mountain to gather firewood, he used twigs to etch his pictures in the earth. When he sat beside the river, he dipped his finger in the water and traced shapes on the nearby rocks. In the cave where he lived, he used pieces of chalk to sketch illustrations over its walls.

Ma Liang practiced his painting everyday. And each day his drawing became more lifelike. It was not long before his birds seemed about to take flight; his fish seemed wet and salty from the sea. But still Ma Liang yearned for a paintbrush of his own.

Then one night Ma Liang had a most wondrous dream. He dreamed that a wrinkled, ancient man stood before him. In his hand he held the most magnificent paintbrush Ma Liang had ever seen or dared imagine. Its bristles were the color of fresh honey and its handle was decorated with enough gold and gems to feed the people of Clear Glade for over a hundred years.

"This is a magic brush," said the ancient man. "Because of your love of the mountain and its inhabitants, the spirits have given it to you. But beware, it must be used carefully."

Ma Liang took the dazzling brush in his hand. "Thank you, grandfather," he started to say, but before he could finish the old man had vanished. Ma Liang woke with a start. "So it was but a dream," Ma Liang thought disappointedly. "I have been listening to the village tales for too long." But just then a glint of gold caught Ma Liang's eye. Sure enough, the magic brush lay at the foot of his wooden bed.

Excitedly, Ma Liang took up the brush and began to paint on the walls of his cave. No sooner had he finished painting a huge bird than it spread its wings and soared high into the air. No sooner had he finished painting a long shiny fish than it frisked its glimmering tail, dodged out of the cave and plunged into the nearby stream. So the brush was magic! It made painted things become real. With such a brush as this Ma Liang could help the people of Clear Glade. He could give them the tools they needed to work and live more comfortably. So the next day Ma Liang went into the village and painted a hoe for one family, an oil lamp for another. The people of Clear Glade could not believe their good fortune, and they thanked both Ma Liang and the spirits of Feather Mountain.

But such strange happenings as this could not remain secret for long. Neighbor told neighbor, stranger told stranger, and soon the village's most greedy and powerful landlord learned of the magic brush. "Bring me that orphan boy and his magic brush!" he yelled to his servants and they obediently went to Ma Liang's cave, bound the boy, and carried him to their master's house on the outskirts of town.

"Paint for me!" ordered the mighty landlord. But Ma Liang would not paint. "Lock him in the stable and do not send him food!" ordered the greedy landlord and Ma Liang was dragged away.

For three days it snowed and for three days no food was taken to Ma Liang. On the fourth day the landlord went to the stable. He was certain that he would find Ma Liang dead from cold and starvation. But as he approached the prison-stable, he smelled freshly cooked hotcakes. Peering through a crack in the door, he saw Ma Liang looking as strong as ever. He was standing beside a burning stove, warming himself as piles of hotcakes cooked on the burner. Ma Liang had painted himself both food and a stove.

The landlord pulled at his thin mustache and shook

his small head. Then he yelled for his men to kill Ma Liang and seize the magic brush.

A dozen of the landlord's fiercest men rushed into the stable, but Ma Liang was no longer there. A ladder now leaned against the wall. Ma Liang had painted his own escape! The landlord rushed up the ladder. But the rungs gave way right from under him and he fell noisily to the ground. By the time he was on his feet again, the ladder had disappeared and the stable was empty once more.

Ma Liang had used his brush to escape from the landlord's house, but he was far from safe. He knew that the powerful landlord would not let himself lose face by being so easily fooled by a peasant boy. No, he would search for Ma Liang until he found him, no matter how long that took. So Ma Liang painted himself a quick horse, mounted it, and waved farewell to Feather Mountain, whose spirits had given him his magic brush.

The orphan boy had not traveled long before he heard the sound of many horses close on his trail. Looking back, he could see the landlord of Clear Glade riding a huge white horse, a shining sword waving furiously in his hand. Behind him rode a score of servants, each carrying a blazing torch to light the way.

Ma Liang calmly pulled out the magic brush. He painted a bow and arrow in the air and then sent an arrow sailing toward the greedy landlord. An instant later the landlord lay dead upon the ground. Ma Liang coaxed his horse on—faster and faster—until at last it seemed to fly as if on wings.

Ma Liang did not stop for food or drink for several days and nights. Finally he came to a distant land where they had never heard of the greedy landlord or Ma Liang and his magic brush. This is where he decided to settle. The mountains weren't as steep or as green as his beloved Feather Mountain, and he did not know if the spirits would be as kind to him here as they had been in Clear Glade. But it seemed far from danger. The people weren't as poor here as they were in Clear Glade, and so Ma Liang decided to earn his living painting pictures to sell at the local market. But he had to take care. He could not let his creations come to life. Such strange occurrences would surely make his whereabouts known. So Ma Liang was careful to leave his paintings incomplete. He painted his birds without beaks or eyes, his animals without legs, his fish without gills.

One day Ma Liang painted a beautiful blue and white bird. He was very careful to paint the bird without eyes. But just as he was about to roll up the painting, some ink splattered onto the paper—exactly where the eyes should have been. The bird flapped his wide wings and flew off in full view of the entire town. It was only a matter of days before the news of this miracle had spread. It was only a matter of weeks before the emperor himself had come to hear of Ma Liang and his magic brush.

There was no one in the land as greedy as the emperor, not even the landlord of Clear Glade. The emperor sent scores of men to capture Ma Liang and bring him and the magic brush to court. Ma Liang tried to resist, he fought and kicked the emperor's men, but there were many and he was but one.

The emperor's palace towered high into the skies. Its walls and ceilings were painted gold and green and red. Huge lions—symbols of the Han ruler's might—were carved in stone at the grand entrance. Inside sat the emperor on a throne of ivory and gold. He wore a robe embroidered in gold and silk. Beside him sat the empress, princesses, princes, court officials and ministers. They all looked on as the emperor commanded Ma Liang to paint.

"Paint me a phoenix!" he commanded Ma Liang. But Ma Liang painted a cock instead.

"Paint me the sacred dragon!" he ordered Ma Liang. But Ma Liang painted a toad. The ugly toad and the filthy cock leaped and flapped all around, leaving dirt and droppings everywhere. The emperor of all China seized the magic brush and ordered his men to imprison poor Ma Liang.

Then the emperor himself began to paint. First he painted a gold mountain. But he was not satisfied with a single mountain of gold. So he painted another and another until there was an entire mountain range. Just as he was standing back to admire his work, a loud noise filled the palace. Slowly the mountains turned to rock and the rock began to crumble, nearly crushing the emperor and his entourage.

But the emperor's mind was filled with visions of great wealth. He would not stop his folly. So he painted a gold brick. This he thought was also too small. So he painted it bigger and bigger. But each time he was not satisfied. Finally he painted a long, golden bar. The moment he finished, a hissing sound began to fill the hall. The long bar began to slither and slide. At its end a huge crimson mouth appeared. The giant snake was just about to bite the emperor when his servants dragged it away.

Fear of poisonous venom or weighty avalanches did not deter the ruler of China. He knew now that only Ma Liang could paint with the magic brush. He had the boy released from prison and spoke to him sweetly with promises of wealth and fame. And so Ma Liang finally agreed to paint for the emperor.

The emperor pondered a long time over what to have Ma Liang paint. "If he paints a mountain, wild beasts such as the huge snake might attack me again," he thought. "No, I shall be smart and have him paint me the calm sea."

So Ma Liang took up his magic brush and painted a clear sea. Its surface was unruffled and it shone like an immense jade mirror.

"Why are there no fish in this sea?" asked the emperor.

Ma Liang drew a few dots with his magic brush.

Suddenly there appeared fish of every color. They frisked their tails and swam about before slowly heading out to sea.

The emperor watched them with the greatest pleasure. As they swam further and further away he urged Ma Liang:

"Hurry up and paint a boat! I want to sail out to sea to watch those fish!"

Ma Liang painted a huge sailing boat with sails the color of fresh milk. The emperor and his empress, the princesses and the princes, the officials and the ministers all boarded the large sailing boat.

Then with a few quick strokes, Ma Liang drew a wind. Fine ripples appeared on the sea and the boat moved off.

But the emperor found the pace too slow. Standing on the bow he shouted:

"Let the wind blow harder! Harder!"

A few powerful strokes from Ma Liang's brush and the wind grew stronger. Clouds began to grow dark and the sea became rough. The milk-white sails billowed out as the boat sailed swiftly toward mid-ocean.

Ma Liang drew a few more strokes. The wind roared, waves rolled and the boat began to keel.

"That's enough wind!" shouted the emperor. "Enough I say!"

But Ma Liang did not reply. He wielded his magic brush back and forth, back and forth. Its golden handle shimmered and gleamed. The sea lashed in fury and splashed against the rocking boat.

The greedy emperor clung to the mast, his fine clothes dripping with sea water, his fist shaking furiously at Ma Liang.

But Ma Liang did not stop. Faster and faster were his strokes now. A hurricane began to blow. Waves beat down onto the boat. Finally, it keeled over and the raging sea swallowed it up like a starving beast. In a moment there were no more emperor, empress, princes, princesses, officials, or ministers. The sea was calm and still once more.

And what became of the orphan boy named Ma Liang? Some say he returned to the village of Clear Glade and the mountain he always loved. Still others say that he roamed the earth and helped the poor by painting for them with his magic brush.

THE STONEMASON

---

a T'ung folktale

*T*HERE was once a Han stonemason who lived close to the T'ung people. He was a fine craftsman and well-respected by them.

Then one day a rich merchant needed a large stone cut. And so he called for the Han stonemason. When the mason came to the merchant's house, his eyes were wide in wonder. Never had he seen such a fine place, never had he seen such elegant robes or smelled such wonderful smells. After he left, the stonemason could think of little else. Oh, how he longed to be a wealthy man!

And a fairy heard the stonemason's wish and she granted it. And from then on the mason was a rich man. And he was happier than he had ever been.

Then a high official passed through the mason's small village. He was carried in an embroidered sedan by foot soldiers who banged on gongs and drums to warn all that an important man was passing and they must bow. And when he did pass, all bowed low. But the stonemason thought to himself, "Why should I bow to this high official? Don't I have just as many servants?" And so he did not bow.

But no one had ever affronted the high official in this way. He ordered the defiant stonemason bound, lashed and fined.

And when the high official and his foot soldiers were far away, the stonemason rose painfully from the ground. He sighed a great sigh and thought to himself, "How powerful must be the high official that all should be forced to bow before him. He must be more powerful than a rich merchant." And from then on he longed only to be a high official.

And the fairy heard him again, and granted his wish. The stonemason became a high official and he was happier than he had ever been.

Now the mason rode about in a fine embroidered sedan. Wherever he went he made sure his foot soldiers banged their drums and gongs loudly. And wherever he went he made the people bow, and he was greatly hated.

One day he and his men passed by a group of lovely T'ung maidens. The mason and his men began to taunt and torment them. The girls shouted and screamed for help. Their cries could be heard far into the distance. It was not long before the surrounding hills were covered with angry T'ung tribesmen each carrying an axe or hoe. They attacked the stonemason and his men, captured and bound them and dragged them back to the village. And each was given a thrashing before being set free.

The stonemason's back stung from the whip for some time thereafter. But he did not continue his evildoing. Instead he thought of the T'ung tribesmen and how brave and strong they were. "Officials do not frighten the T'ung people," he thought admiringly. "Nothing and no one rules over them." And from then on he longed only to be a T'ung tribesman.

And once again the fairy heard his wish and granted it. And the stonemason was so happy that he laughed and smiled all day.

Each morning he went to the hillside where he worked beside the other tribesmen till late into the day. The scorching sun blazed down on their backs. So hot was the sun that the birds and the animals hid in the mountain forests. The water buffaloes buried themselves deep in the thick slimy mud. Only the young, tender rice sprouts stood up to the sun—as unyielding as the T'ung people themselves. The stonemason looked up at the scorching sun and he thought, "The sun must rule over the entire universe. It is surely the most powerful of all." And from then on he longed only to be the powerful sun.

The fairy heard his wish and turned the mason into the sun. He was delighted and beamed his fierce rays down on the earth and its people. He wilted the flowers and burned the grass. He made people sweat and animals pant. All day long he beat down on the earth and its creatures and took joy in the misery he caused.

But then a black cloud came whistling out of the west. In moments it had covered up the sun and its powerful rays. The earth below became shaded and cool. And so the mason thought, "Who would have imagined that a black cloud could be more powerful than the blazing sun!" And from then on the stonemason longed only to be a great black cloud.

Again the fairy heard his wish and turned the stonemason into a great black cloud. And the stonemason was happier than ever before.

All day he glided across the sky, delighting in blocking the sun's fierce rays. He caused great pounding rains to pour upon the land, flooding crops and fields in its wake. He caused the rivers to overflow and huts and mansions alike to be washed away. He made lightning flash across the sky and thunder deafen the ear. Nothing could possibly be fiercer and more powerful than a great black cloud.

But then one day a sudden gust of wind came whistling and howling out of the east. It blew the black cloud apart. "How powerful is the wind!" exclaimed the stonemason. "Who would have thought it even mightier than a great black cloud." And from then on he longed only to be a gust of wind.

And the fairy heard his wish and turned him into a fierce wind. And the stonemason was delighted.

All day long he blew like a mighty typhoon. He uprooted trees, overturned houses, destroyed whole villages. He whistled and howled so much that people were afraid to leave their homes for fear of being blown right off their feet. How powerful and fierce he was!

Then while he was blowing over the land he came to a huge stone boulder. He blew with all his force, but the stone did not budge. And so the stonemason thought to himself, "The wind is certainly fierce, but it is powerless against stone. Oh, to be a huge stone boulder! No one and nothing can dominate a rock!"

And the fairy, having heard his wish, turned the mason into a boulder sitting high up on a mountaintop. And the stonemason felt that he could not be happier than this.

All day long he sat in his tall lookout, reveling in his strength and size. Below, the villagers replanted their crops, rebuilt their huts, dammed up their rivers. How small and insignificant they seemed.

Then he heard the sound of a chisel, hacking away at the huge stone boulder, and suddenly the stonemason was afraid. He begged the fairy to tell him what to do.

"You have been many powerful things," she said softly. "But perhaps it is best to be a stonemason after all." With that she turned him back into his former self. And the stonemason was happier than he had ever been.